Herbs have be by Mankind fo

GH00888928

In ancient times, Egyptian Pharaohs were entombed with all they required for the after-life, including a good selection of medicinal plants. The Greeks and Romans used herbs extensively, developing one of the earliest systems of medicine and recording the usage of many herbs. Further to the East, the Chinese developed their form of herbal medicine alongside acupuncture and the Indians worked on a system, known as Ayurvedic medicine, encompassing many types of herbs.

In recent years in the West herbs have been the starting material for many of the pharmaceutical medicines that we know today. Digoxin was first used as the plant Digitalis and Aspirin was first isolated from the bark of the Willow.

Despite the advances of modern healthcare and medicine, it is quite clear to many people that plant medicine, or Phytotherapy, still plays a very important part in the health of everyone in our 21st Century world.

For many ailments, we do not need to resort to 'strong' drugs, when the gentler action of herbs can do the work. One clear example is the use of antibiotics for the common cold, when the action of Echinacea makes so much more sense. The action of many herbs has now been confirmed and proven through research and clinical trials.

This small handbook looks at a selection of herbs most commonly used in the West to give you an idea of how they can improve and maintain your health. It is not intended to replace medical advice. You should consult a healthcare practitioner if you have any condition which is of concern. Also it is recommended that you consult a doctor or pharmacist before taking herbal remedies if you are pregnant or breastfeeding.

AESCULUS

Also known as: Aesculus hippocastanum semen, Horse Chestnut seed.

Uses: Varicose veins, Haemorrhoids.

Description: The use of Aesculus in venous disorders has been recognised for a long time and it has been used as a treatment for various venous conditions since the 19th Century.

It is the seed of the Horse Chestnut tree, instantly recognisable to many children as the 'Conker', that is used medicinally. A commonly held belief in the 18th Century was that carrying Horse Chestnut seeds 'in one's pocket' would prevent gout, rheumatism and back pain. There does not seem to be much evidence to support this in modern research.

How it works: The constituent of Aesculus which has been most studied is Aescin. It has the ability to improve the tone of veins, reducing leakage into the surrounding tissue.

Often varicose veins are more troublesome in the summer and starting a course of Aesculus during the early summer can prevent the distressing symptoms during the warmer weather. For best results, I find that a three to four month course is advisable. Those suffering from varicose veins will also benefit from ensuring that constipation is not a factor.

When to avoid: Do not use if taking anticoagulants such as Warfarin. Do not use if pregnant or breastfeeding.

AGNUS CASTUS

Also known as: Chaste Tree, Vitex agnus castus.

Uses: Premenstrual Syndrome (PMS), Teenage acne.

Description: This herb has a long tradition of use as a general 'balancer' for the female hormones. Despite its common name, Chaste Tree, Agnus castus is actually a shrub found in the Mediterranean. The fruit of the plant is used in Phytotherapy and gives off a pleasant peppermint-like smell.

How it works: Agnus castus acts on the Pituitary gland to increase the secretion of Luteinising Hormone, which leads to an increase in the production of progesterone during the second half of the menstrual cycle. It has also been reported to possess the ability to inhibit Prolactin.

Both these actions are thought to be important in PMS, particularly as many who suffer with the problem have a greater sensitivity to Prolactin. Agnus castus has also been found to be beneficial in the treatment of acne in both men and women.

When to avoid: Seek advice from a healthcare practitioner if using oral contraceptives or HRT. Do not use if pregnant or breastfeeding.

ALLIUM SATIVUM

Also known as: Garlic.

Uses: High cholesterol.

Description: Garlic is one of the more commonly used health supplements in the world. It is said to be the world's second oldest medicine after Ephedra and is still one of the best and most popular herbal remedies.

Remains of Garlic have been found in caves inhabited 10,000 years ago. A Sumerian clay tablet dating from 3,000 BC records the first garlic prescription.

How it works: It is now recognised that it is the ratio of the various types of cholesterol and fats in the blood which is more relevant than the totals measured. Whilst Garlic lowers the levels of cholesterol and triglycerides, it reduces the level of low density lipoproteins (LDL) whilst increasing the levels of high density lipoproteins (HDL). It has been suggested that an increase in HDL may enhance removal of cholesterol.

Garlic also has a mild action in lowering blood pressure and possesses antioxidant activity.

When to avoid: No restrictions on use are known.

ALOE VERA

Also known as: Aloe barbadensis.

Uses: Healing of wounds and burns, Psoriasis.

Description: Aloe vera has been used in wound healing for thousands of years. The Egyptians used it in 1,500 BC for skin problems and infections. The Greek physician Dioscorides recommended it externally for wounds, haemorrhoids, ulcers and hair loss.

The plant has thick fleshy leaves that contain a clear gel and is easy to grow indoors.

How it works: The plant contains anthraquinone glycosides, resins and polysacharrides.

When taken internally, Aloe vera has a 'cleansing' effect on the body, by virtue of its action on the digestive tract. This makes it useful for a number of skin conditions, especially psoriasis, where the process of internal detoxification is deemed by naturopaths to be important.

Scientific use of Aloe in wound healing was first documented in 1935. Since then, there have been a number of studies showing its effectiveness as a treatment for burns and other wounds.

When to avoid: Aloe vera can have a laxative effect. Do not use if pregnant or breastfeeding.

ARTICHOKE

Also known as: Globe Artichoke, Cynara scolymus.

Uses: Reduces cholesterol levels, Stimulates liver function, Protects the liver, Helps metabolise fats.

Description: Artichokes grow easily in the warmer Mediterranean climate. It is often found as part of the diet of those living in these countries and considered to be a luxury food. Like Milk Thistle, the plant belongs to the daisy family. It grows to a height of about 2 metres, producing large violet flowers.

Artichokes have a bitter taste due to the presence of Cynaropicrin, which is found only in the green parts of the plant.

How it works: Apart from Cynaropicrin which stimulates liver function through its 'bitterness', artichokes contain another valuable substance known as Cynarin. This has very specific properties, protecting and enhancing liver function in a way similar to Silymarin which is found in Milk Thistle.

Artichokes also contain a group of compounds known as phenolic acids which have the ability to reduce blood cholesterol and lipid levels through an action on the liver.

When to avoid: Medical opinion should be sought when acute or chronic liver conditions are present.

AVENA SATIVA

Also known as: Oats.

Uses: Tonic for the nerves.

Description: Oats have been used traditionally as a 'nerve tonic' for hundreds of years. It is the seed which is used medicinally and also for food.

How it works: Fresh oat seed contains high levels of vitamin B, minerals and other nutrients. These are recognised to be important and beneficial for the proper functioning of the nervous system. Oats contain a group of substances which have a calming effect on the nervous system, the most active of which, Gramine, has been shown to relax muscles, The balance of constituents present in oat seed probably accounts for the 'restorative' benefits in depression, states of debility and exhaustion — and the traditional use as a Nerve Tonic.

Some researchers have found that oats can be beneficial for those who are trying to overcome the symptoms of withdrawal from alcohol and drugs.

When to avoid: No restrictions on use are known.

BERBERIS

Also known As: Barberry, Berberis vulgaris.

Uses: Gall-stones, Liver tonic.

Description: Berberis vulgaris is a perennial shrub, native to Europe. The leaves and berries are used medicinally.

How it works: Berberis contains the alkaloid berberine, the most well studied of the constituents. It is a powerful antibacterial, effective against disease-bearing micro-organisms such as Salmonella and E. Coli, making it effective in treating the majority of gastrointestinal infections. In addition to this, Berberine stimulates the secretion of bile and bilirubin, supporting its use for gall-stones, obstructive jaundice and sluggish digestive problems.

When to avoid: Those with low blood pressure should seek medical advice before using this herb. Do not use if pregnant or breastfeeding.

BILBERRY

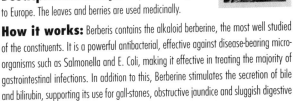

Also known as: Vaccinium myrtillus, European blueberry.

Uses: Eye strain, Improves vision.

Description: Bilberry is a shrub which grows in woods and forests throughout Europe. The fruit is blue-black or purple and has a high nutritive value. It has been used for many years as a general tonic for the eyes. It is said that RAF pilots were encouraged to eat bilberries to improve night vision.

How it works: The main constituents of Bilberries are known as anthocyanosides — a group of flavonoids.

These have the ability to bind to the part of the retina which is responsible for vision, which in turn increases the rate of regeneration of the visual pigments in the retina.

In addition, the substances present in Bilberry have the ability to prevent the destruction of collagen, which is responsible for stabilising the delicate tissue structure of the eyes.

One particular anthocyanidin, Myrtillin, has been shown to reduce blood sugar levels.

When to avoid: No restrictions to use are known.

BLACK COHOSH

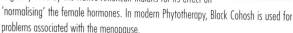

Also known as: Cimicifuga racemosa.

Uses: Menopausal symptoms.

Description: This is a member of the Buttercup family, originally used by the Native American Indians for its effect on 'normalising' the female hormones. In modern Phytotherapy, Black Cohosh is used for problems associated with the menopause.

How it works: The mode of action of Black Cohosh in the treatment of menopausal difficulties is not clear. It seems to act both directly on the tissues of the reproductive system and indirectly through the nervous system.

Black Cohosh contains several important constituents. One group of constituents acts to reduce the concentration of Luteinising Hormone which, in turn, decreases the relative balance of progesterone in favour of the oestrogens. At the same time, another group has been found to act directly on oestrogen receptors.

It provides a natural source of salicylic acid. This may account for some of the beneficial effects seen with painful menstruation during menopause.

When to avoid: Do not use if allergic to Aspirin. Consult a healthcare practitioner before use if you are taking oral contraceptives, HRT or Tamoxifen. Do not use if pregnant or breastfeeding.

CALENDULA

Also known as: Marigold, Calendula officinalis.

Uses: Psoriasis, Eczema, Dermatitis, Wound healing.

Description: Marigold is a common garden plant with a long tradition in European Phytotherapy as a treatment for a variety of skin conditions.

How it works: The active constituents in Calendula officinalis have still to be identified although phytochemical studies have reported flavonoids, volatile oil, carotenoids and triterpenes. The triterpenes appear to be the main active group. The flavonoids may contribute to the anti-inflammatory effect.

When to avoid: Do not use if pregnant or breastfeeding.

CENTAURIUM

Also known as: Centaurium umbellatum, Centaury.

Uses: Acid stomach, Indigestion, Hiatus hernia, Anorexia, Heartburn (reflux).

Description: Centaurium has been used as the classic stomach bitter for many years. Bitter herbs or bitter tasting foods used to form a significant part of the diet. Nowadays, these have practically disappeared with the trend towards more convenient, inoffensive and easy to eat foods.

How it works: As you may have surmised, Centaurium has a bitter taste and owes this property to the group of compounds called bitter glycosides.

The bitterness of food on the tongue plays a very important role in the digestive process. The taste of bitter foods stimulates the appetite and triggers the secretion of digestive juices in the stomach, which in turn improves the breakdown of food.

At the same time, the hormone Gastrin is secreted by the walls of the stomach. This improves the digestive process, by improving the passage of food from the stomach to the intestines. Another important action of Gastrin is to tighten the 'valve' between the oesophagus and stomach, which is important in reducing the symptoms associated with a hiatus hernia, such as gastric reflux.

When to avoid: No restrictions on use are known.

CRATAEGUS

Also known as: Crataegus oxyacantha, Hawthorn.

Uses: Heart tonic.

Description: Hawthorn is a small spiny tree or shrub which is native to Europe. It is often seen growing in hedges. Hawthorn berries have been used by Phytotherapists as a 'heart tonic' for many years.

How it works: Crataegus is perhaps one of the most widely used herbs for the heart. The precise mode of action is still unclear — although we do know that the plant does not contain digitalis-like compounds.

Flavonoids found in Crataegus have been found to improve the circulation of the heart and, to a lesser extent, the circulation of other parts of the body. Glycosides present are believed to increase the tone of the heart, improving the force of contraction whilst reducing the rate of contraction — in short, making the heart work more efficiently.

When to avoid: Let your healthcare practitioner know if you are using Crataegus in addition to any other prescribed medication for the heart.

DANDELION

Also known as: Taraxacum.

Uses: Diuretic, Liver and gall-bladder problems.

Description: The Dandelion plant is often seen as a weed. However, it has distinct medicinal properties and its action on the liver and gall-bladder has been particularly prized by herbalists.

How it works: Dandelion is an excellent cleansing agent, being one of the most effective detoxifying herbs. It possesses a wide range of active constituents and is also rich in minerals and nutrients. The plant stimulates liver and particularly gall-bladder function. This has a primary use in improving digestion as a result of an increase in digestive juices. In addition, Dandelion has diuretic and mild laxative properties.

When to avoid: Those taking diuretics or with liver complaints, gall-stones or an obstructed bile duct should firstly consult their healthcare practitioner.

DEVIL'S CLAW

Also known as: Harpagophytum.

Uses: Anti-inflammatory, Arthritis, Rheumatism, Auto-immune disorders, Allergies, Sports injuries.

Description: This plant is native to the Southern parts of Africa. It is the tubers (or the storage roots) of the plant, measuring approximately 20 cm in length, which are used medicinally.

Devil's Claw is a traditional remedy for general joint pains.

How it works: Devil's Claw contains a group of components known as Iridoids which possess anti-inflammatory, antirheumatic and pain killing properties. The anti-inflammatory action has been shown to be equivalent to that of Steroids, but the plant itself does not seem to contain this group of compounds.

Recent research has shown that the plant has an action in balancing the Immune system, reducing the tendency for allergies and autoimmunity (where the body's immune system attacks normal healthy body cells).

When to avoid: No restrictions on use are known.

ECHINACEA

Also known as: Echinacea purpurea, Purple Coneflower.

Uses: Immune stimulant, Colds, Flu, Healing of wounds and other minor infections.

Description: The Echinacea herb is one of the most popular herbs used in Europe. It is considered to be the prime remedy for the Immune system and this view has been supported by extensive research. The American Indians were the first to recognise the value of the plant, using it for wound healing and snakebites.

How it works: Echinacea works principally by stimulating a group of cells in the Immune system known as the macrophages. These cells have the unique ability to 'eat' matter foreign to the body, such as viruses, bacteria and other particulate matter such as dust particles entering the body as a result of air pollution.

Stimulating the Immune system in this way improves the way that the body handles infections, when viruses and bacteria do manage to invade the body. Whilst there are two other species of Echinacea which may be found in use, tests have shown that Echinacea purpurea has the greatest activity.

Clinical trials have shown that Echinacea can improve the symptoms of colds and flu, shortening the course of the illness in 78% of people.

When to avoid: No restrictions on use are known.

ELEUTHEROCOCCUS

Also known as: Eleutherococcus senticosus, Siberian Ginseng.

Uses: General tonic, Fatigue, Post Viral Fatigue Syndrome.

Description: The root of the herb commonly referred to simply as Eleutherococcus, is an example of an 'Adaptogen'. This has been defined as a substance which enables the body's metabolism to adapt and cope with unfavourable conditions, such as physical and psychological stress, infections and environmental pollutants.

Eleutherococcus is native to Eastern Asia and particularly Siberia. It bears many similar actions to the more familiar Panax Ginseng.

How it works: A group of compounds isolated from Eleutherococcus called the 'Eleutherosides', which include naturally-occurring steroids, are thought to represent the main active constituents. These have a wide range of activities, which support the body's many processes, giving a revitalising effect. In addition, polysaccharides present have been found to possess the ability to stimulate the Immune system.

When to avoid: Those who suffer from hypertension, anxiety, schizophrenia, heart disorders, nervous disorders, diabetes and those taking the contraceptive pill or HRT should first consult a healthcare practitioner .

EUPHRASIA

Also known as: Eyebright.

Uses: Conjunctivitis, Hayfever.

Description: Euphrasia is a small annual plant, native to Britain and Europe. It grows to a height of about 30 cm and bears pale lilac flowers. It has been used as far back as the 17th Century for healthcare. Milton, in his poem *Paradise Lost,* describes how the Archangel Michael used 'Euphrasy' to clear Adam's sight.

How it works: Euphrasia contains a number of active constituents, including Aucubin, caffeic acid and tannins. This last group of compounds work as anti-inflammatory agents, helping to dry up secretions of the mucous membranes.

This is particularly relevant when we consider the most important role of Euphrasia — to reduce the inflammation of the delicate mucous membranes of the eyes (conjunctivitis) when they are afflicted by infections or allergy (hayfever). The preparation should be taken internally.

When to avoid: Do not use Euphrasia externally.

FEVERFEW

Also known as: Tanacetum parthenium.

Uses: Migraine headaches.

Description: Feverfew has daisy-like flowers, a characteristic of the Compositae family to which it belongs. It is a plant which is commonly found in temperate climes and, traditionally, those suffering from migraine headaches were advised to place a leaf from the feverfew plant in their sandwich!

How it works: Feverfew has been subject to a fair amount of research. Sesquiterpene lactones are thought to be the main active constituents of the plant. They inhibit platelet aggregation and the secretion of serotonin, which is one of the substances released during a migraine headache.

When to avoid: Some people may be prone to mouth ulcers when using Feverfew.

GALEOPSIS

Also known as: Hemp Nettle.

Uses: Stress incontinence, Supportive treatment in asthma.

Description: Hemp Nettle is a member of the Labiatae family, a group of plants commonly found in Germany.

How it works: Galeopsis contains a large amount of silica, saponins and tannins. The silicic acid content increases non-specific lung resistance to allergies and pathogens through a temporary increase in white blood cells.

Silica is also of great importance in the regeneration of tissue. High concentrations are normally found in the trachea and lung tissue. Levels decrease with the presence of respiratory disease when the requirement becomes greater.

Saponins present have an expectorant action which enhances the expulsion of phlegm from the lungs.

Galeopsis is also useful for stress incontinence and bedwetting through the astringent action of tannins in 'toning up' tissue.

When to avoid: Do not stop prescribed medication when using Galeopsis without the knowledge of your doctor.

GINGER

Also known as: Zingiber officinalis.

Uses: Motion sickness, Morning sickness, Poor circulation

Description: This is another example of how our food is also our medicine. The Ginger plant is native to South East Asia, where it is used extensively in cooking. A traditional food to fortify pregnant women in these countries is chicken soup heavily laced with Ginger.

How it works: Ginger contains a number of substances, many of which are volatile oils. As a digestive tonic, Ginger improves the production and secretion of bile, aids fat breakdown and lowers blood cholesterol levels. This speeds up the digestive processes, allowing quicker transport of substances through the digestive tract, lessening the irritation in the intestines, reducing flatulence and intestinal spasms.

When to avoid: Some people may experience heartburn or be sensitive to the taste of Ginger.

GINKGO BILOBA

Also known as: Memory Tree, Maidenhair Tree.

Uses: Improves arterial circulation, Improves memory.

Description: This is probably one of the oldest medicinal
herbs known to Man. Its use can be traced to the oldest Chinese
Materia Medica dating back to around 3,000 BC. Traditional Chinese medicine describes
the ability of Ginkgo leaves to 'benefit the brain'. Today, Ginkgo extracts are among the
most widely prescribed Phytomedicines in both Germany and France. In Germany alone,
10 million prescriptions for Ginkgo are written each year by more than 10,000 physicians.

How it works: The action of Ginkgo has been quite clearly demonstrated in
various research tests. Direct action on the arterial circulation increases the blood flow
through these vessels. At the same time, the herb has been shown to inhibit a substance
known as Platelet Activating Factor (PAF) which further improves blood flow whilst acting
as an anti-inflammatory agent. Ginkgo has also been shown to have anti-oxidant effects,
which are important in stabilising cell membranes in the body.

When to avoid: Consult your healthcare practitioner if using Aspirin or Warfarin.

HOPS

Also known as: Humulus lupulus.

Uses: Insomnia, Nervous tension.

Description: The plant Humulus is a climber which can
be found in swamps and in the hedges of our cultivated gardens.
Being an important ingredient in beer, it is extensively cultivated commercially. Hops have
a long history of use in Phytotherapy. It was listed in the US *Pharmacopoeia* from 1831
to 1916 as a sedative.

How it works: Hops contain substances known as Humulones and Lupulones.
These are broken down in the body to substances which have a distinct sedative effect on
the nervous system. This effect is extremely useful especially when combined with the
herb Valerian, for insomnia, or when there is an element of nervous tension/anxiety
involved.

When to avoid: No restrictions on use are known.

HYPERICUM

Also known as: St John's Wort.

Uses: Depression, Neuralgia, Sciatica, Shingles.

Description: This herb is the traditional remedy for depression. It is commonly found in temperate countries and has recently gained immense popularity as a herb used in healthcare.

How it works: There is little doubt that Hypericum works by influencing the neurotransmitters in the brain. The substances responsible for this action are now known to be Hypericin and more recently, Hyperforin. However, it is widely accepted that the action of the herb cannot be assigned to a specific constituent but is rather the balanced effect of all the substances within the plant.

Hypericum has also been found to contain flavonoids which possess analgesic action in those suffering with neuralgia – the most common of which is sciatica.

When to avoid: Please check with your doctor/pharmacist or healthcare practitioner if you are taking any prescribed medicines as Hypericum may affect the way they work.

IVY

Also known as: Hedera helix.

Uses: Coughs, Expectorant.

Description: The Common Ivy is a plant which can be found easily in our gardens. It is a climbing plant and it is the leaves which are used medicinally.

How it works: Ivy is an example of a herb which has an expectorant action on the chest, elicited by a reflex action in the stomach, due to its saponin content. It loosens the mucus from the tubes of the lungs, encouraging its expulsion and elimination. Often troublesome coughs indicate difficulty in eliminating mucus and a herb such as Ivy, in thinning mucus, helps to clear the chest.

The action of Ivy in this type of cough is enhanced particularly when Thyme is added.

When to avoid: No restrictions on use are known.

KAVA-KAVA

Also known as: Piper methysticum.

Uses: Anxiety, Insomnia, Relieving muscle tension, Tension headaches.

Description: This plant is a perennial shrub belonging to the pepper family and can be found in nearly all of the Pacific Islands. Kava has a significant role in the culture of these islands and plays an important part in traditional ceremonies. Traditionally the herb is used to induce 'calm'. Overindulgence of the herb can produce euphoria and intoxication.

How it works: The active components of Kava-kava are known as kava lactones. These substances have the ability to reduce anxiety by acting on certain areas of the brain, blocking sodium channels, which in turn decrease nerve activity.

Studies have demonstrated that Kava-kava is a safe and non-addictive agent to be used for anxiety. Although it has a different mode of activity, its effectiveness is comparable to that of the Benzodiazepine class of drugs such as Valium. Kava-kava also appears to be an effective pain killer and this is coupled with its ability to relax muscle.

When to avoid: Should not be taken at the same time as alcohol. Consult your healthcare practitioner before using with drugs for the nervous system. Long term use should be approved by your practitioner.

KELP

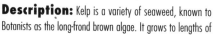

Also known as: Macrocystis pyrifera.

Uses: Stimulates metabolism, Obesity, Detoxification.

Description: Kelp is a variety of seaweed, known to Botanists as the long-frond brown algae. It grows to lengths of up to 60 metres in the temperate parts of the Pacific and Atlantic Oceans. This plant used to play an important part in the culture of fishing communities where it was used for fuel and food. However, apart from Japan, the use of seaweed has faded out.

How it works: Kelp is rich in Iodine. It also contains Bromine, trace elements and vitamin A. The main activity of Kelp lies with its Iodine content. It is an important component of thyroid hormones, which play a major part in regulating the body's metabolism. Increasing the Iodine available to the body will increase the level of activity in the thyroid gland, raising the body's general metabolism. Kelp also contains substances known as alginates. These molecules have the unique property of being able to absorb onto their surfaces heavy metals, radioactive substances and organic molecules such as cholesterol.

When to avoid: Kelp is not advised for anyone with high blood pressure, kidney disorders or thyroid conditions, unless taken under medical supervision. Certain people may also be allergic to Iodine, and hence, Kelp. Do not use if pregnant or breastfeeding.

KNOTGRASS

Also known as: Polygonum aviculare.

Uses: Arthritis, Gout, Carpal Tunnel Syndrome

Description: Knotgrass is one of the oldest traditional remedies for arthritis and general inflammatory joint conditions. It appears as a weed in many temperate countries and is difficult to eradicate once established, due to its strong root and runner system below soil level.

How it works: The active substances of this plant have not yet been studied extensively. Knotgrass is known to contain silica, which can help to improve the elasticity and strength of connective tissues in the body and particularly the joints.

In addition, the plant appears to work as an anti-inflammatory agent by helping the body in the elimination of toxins.

When to avoid: No restrictions on use are known.

LINSEED

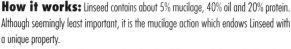

Also known as: Semen linum.

Uses: Laxative.

Description: Linseed is the seed from the plant known as Common Flax (Linum usitatissimum). In the past, flax played a very important part in the economy and culture of communities in which it was grown.

How it works: Linseed contains about 5% mucilage, 40% oil and 20% protein. Although seemingly least important, it is the mucilage action which endows Linseed with a unique property.

In the presence of water, mucilage has the ability to swell, increasing its volume considerably. This 'bulking' ability can be extremely beneficial to the digestive tract when bowel action is slow or 'lazy'. The bulking action relies on water, and hence Linseed should be taken with plenty of fluid.

The oils present in Linseed also act as a lubricant, supporting the bulking action of mucilage.

When to avoid: It is not advisable to use laxative agents on a long term basis without the advice of a healthcare practitioner.

MARUM VERUM

Also known as: Cat's Thyme

Use: Snoring, Nasal polyps.

Description: Marum verum is a small shrub, native to Spain. Its traditional use has been in the form of snuff. The fresh leaves and young branches, when rubbed, give off an aromatic smell that can trigger sneezing.

How it works: The evidence of Marum verum's activity is mainly empirical and derived from clinical experience. It appears to have the ability to reduce inflammation of the nasal passages.

Its ability to reduce snoring could be due to the removal of blockages and better functioning of tissues, membranes and nervous pathways in the nose and throat.

When to avoid: Do not use if pregnant or breastfeeding.

MELISSA

Also known as: Lemon Balm.

Uses: Palpitations, Tension, Anxiety, Insomnia, Nervous digestive disorders.

Description: Melissa is a perennial herb with yellow-green, oval-shaped leaves. Originating in southern Europe, it is now a common garden herb worldwide.

How it works: The essential oil in Melissa has been shown to have antispasmodic and relaxant properties, making the herb particularly useful in the treatment of digestive disorders resulting from nervous tension. Studies on other constituents have revealed antiviral and anti-inflammatory activity.

When to avoid: No restrictions on use are known.

MILK THISTLE

Also known as: Carduus marianus, Silybum marianum.

Uses: Liver function stimulant, Detoxification, Gall-stones, High cholesterol, Liver tonic.

Description: The Milk Thistle is a large plant with glossy, green, spiky leaves bearing conspicuous white veins. The flowers are purple and large. The plant originates from the Mediterranean and it is now cultivated in many parts of Europe as an ornamental plant. Milk Thistle has a long history of use as a medicinal plant. It was previously administered for its bitter properties, but more recently it has been recognised more and more as an excellent remedy for liver complaints.

How it works: The main constituent of Milk Thistle appears to be the substance known as Silymarin. This has the unique function of being able to act directly on the cells of the liver producing a liver-protective effect.

Silymarin has been shown to be able to prevent liver cell damage, through stimulating the enzymatic function of liver cells and encouraging the regeneration of the liver.

All these factors are important in overall health, with the liver acting as the most important avenue for the elimination of toxins found within the body.

When to avoid: Medical opinion should be sought when acute or chronic liver conditions are present.

NEEM

Also known as: Azadirachta indica A. Juss.

Uses: Mild skin infections, Psoriasis, Eczema, Athlete's foot, Ringworm, Head lice, Scabies.

Description: The Neem tree is a member of the mahogany family, originating from the Bay of Bengal. It has been used traditionally for the treatment of many diseases in Ayurvedic medicine and for the protection of people and animals from insect pests.

How it works: The Neem tree contains at least 35 biologically active principles distributed throughout the leaves, seeds and bark.

Neem leaves have antibacterial activity, the constituents nimbolide and nimbic acid have been shown to be active against the bacteria responsible for abscesses and wound infections. In addition, the leaves and the oil from the seeds have anti-inflammatory properties.

The insecticidal properties of Neem oil are due to the constituent Azadirachtin A. It mimics the insect hormonal system and affects feeding, development and reproduction.

When to avoid: Neem should not be taken internally. Diabetics should not self treat any conditions of the foot. Do not use if pregnant or breastfeeding.

PASSIFLORA

Also known as: Passion Flower.

Uses: Anxiety, Insomnia, Nervous tension, Nerve pain, Depression.

Description: Passiflora is a climbing plant, popular in gardens in Europe. It originates from South America and the East Indies and was traditionally used as a nerve tonic in neuralgia. It is used extensively in Homoeopathy.

How it works: Passiflora has a sedative effect on the central nervous system. However, its mode of action is not clear and the active constituents in the plant have not been clearly identified. It was originally thought that the active constituent was the alkaloid known as passiflorine or Harman.

When To avoid: Avoid excessive doses. Do not use if pregnant or breastfeeding.

PEPPERMINT

Also known as: Mentha piperita.

Uses: Irritable Bowel Syndrome.

Description: There are many varieties of Peppermint which can be found. These differ in their medicinal properties, as a result of differing levels of volatile oils.

How it works: Menthol is one of the most prominent of the volatile oils found in Peppermint. The plant as a whole works as a carminative (dispels wind), reducing the symptoms of nausea, colic, bloating and wind. It also relaxes muscle tension in the colon which helps to relieve spasms.

Research has shown that Peppermint is able to relieve the symptoms of Irritable Bowel Syndrome.

When to avoid: No restrictions on use are known.

PETASITES

Also known as: Butterbur.

Uses: Migraine headaches, muscle spasm, period pain, gastric pain.

Description: Butterbur is a member of the daisy family, commonly found in damp woodland areas or growing along riverbanks. The leaves of the plant are very large and round, hence the name Petasites, meaning 'large brimmed hat'.

How it works: Petasites contains the constituent Petasin. This is thought to be the most important active ingredient due to its antispasmodic and pain relieving properties.

Research has shown that these properties are particularly useful both for the treatment and prevention of migraine.

Recent research also suggests that Petasites is useful for the treatment of hayfever and other forms of allergic rhinitis.

When to avoid: Petasites should not be used to treat migraine symptoms that have not been previously diagnosed by a medical practitioner.

PLANTAGO

Also known as: Plantago lanceolata, Ribwort Plantain.

Uses: Ear infections, Glue ear, Upper respiratory tract congestion, Catarrh.

Description: This is a very common plant in Europe, growing in large quantities in dry meadows and fields, where it is easy to find. Plantago, a member of the Plantain family, produces a rosette of slender pointed leaves and a flowering stem which arises from the centre, carrying small flowers.

How it works: Plantago contains mucilage, tannins and silicic acid. It is probably the mucilage which contributes most to the action of the plant as a cough remedy.

Plantago also has the ability to reduce the amount of inflammation present in the mucous membranes of the upper respiratory tract.

It has been noted that Plantain juice will not go mouldy during storage, although large amounts of sugar are present. It has been found that this is due to the presence of naturally occurring antibiotics. This may explain its action in conditions such as middle ear infections and glue ear.

When to avoid: No restrictions on use are known.

SAGE

Also known as: Salvia officinalis.

Uses: Menopausal hot flushes, Sore throats.

Description: Sage is commonly used to enhance the taste of food. The plant is native to the Mediterranean, although it also grows well in temperate climes.

How it works: Sage is one of the plants known as a phyto-oestrogen. In itself, the plant does not contain any oestrogen-like compounds but possesses the potential of influencing oestrogen activity in the body.

In addition, Sage has a separate role in preventing sweating. The combination of these two actions makes Sage an excellent preparation to help with the hot flushes which often accompany the decline in hormonal levels at the time of the menopause.

Sage has also been found to possess antibacterial properties and can be very beneficial for sore throats when used as a gargle.

When to avoid: Consult a healthcare practitioner before use if you are taking oral contraceptives, HRT or Tamoxifen or if you suffer from diabetes or epilepsy.

SAW PALMETTO

Also known as: Sabal serrulata, Serenoa repens.

Uses: Enlarged prostate, Benign Prostatic Hypertrophy.

Description: This is a small palm with fan-shaped leaves. The fruit, which is dark red, is the size of an olive and contains a volatile oil known as Palmetto oil. It is the fruit that is used medicinally.

Saw Palmetto is considered by herbalists to be the prime remedy for prostate problems.

How it works: The condition of an enlarged prostate is commonly found in men over the age of 50. This enlargement is the result of the cells in the prostate becoming more sensitive to circulating hormonal levels in the body. Cells of the prostate enlarge, which in turn cause the whole gland to increase in size.

Saw Palmetto inhibits enzymes at the level of the prostate cells, reducing the action of hormones. This is a local effect, confined to the prostate gland.

When to avoid: Medical advice should be sought if the condition persists or is accompanied by bleeding or a fever.

SOLIDAGO

Also known as: Golden Rod.

Uses: Diuretic, Improves renal function, Kidney tonic.

Description: The herb Solidago is a traditional 'Kidney tonic'. It is a small, herbaceous plant found in temperate countries and often found in the natural flora of grassy mountainous areas.

How it works: Whilst Solidago has diuretic action, this is not the prime role of the plant. Solidago has been shown to have important anti-inflammatory, antispasmodic and antiseptic action and seems to strengthen kidney function.

This makes it useful as an agent to counter inflammation and irritation of the kidneys, when infection or stones are present. The diuretic action is also useful in helping to dissolve kidney stones.

When to avoid: Consult your doctor if the urinary tract condition persists or if accompanied by bleeding, fever, nausea or vomiting.

SPILANTHES

Also known as: Paracress.

Uses: Athlete's foot, Ringworm, Oral thrush, Candidiasis, Thrush.

Description: Spilanthes originates from South America and grows in wet, damp places in temperate climates. It is a member of the Asteraceae family and was traditionally used in Europe for the external treatment of fungal skin infections.

How it works: Spilanthes contains the essential oil Spilanthole which is anti-inflammatory. Studies carried out in the 1950s highlighted the insecticidal properties of the essential oil. Spilanthes also contains tannic acid, a known astringent.

Its main use in the treatment of fungal infections stems more from empirical evidence than clinical research.

When to avoid: Do not use if pregnant or breastfeeding.

THYME

Also known as: Thymus vulgaris, Common Thyme.

Uses: Chest conditions.

Description: This is another herb which is well known for its culinary use. There are many species of Thyme. Common Thyme originates from the Mediterranean and is the most widely used medicinal variety.

How it works: The primary active components of Thyme are the volatile oils, especially Thymol. These act locally on the lungs as they are eliminated from the body through the Respiratory tract, disinfecting the airways, relaxing bronchial spasm and reducing the viscosity of mucus.

These actions help the lungs expel mucus, benefiting bronchitis and chesty catarrhal conditions.

When to avoid: Consult your doctor if blood is present in mucus.

TORMENTIL

Also known as: Potentilla tormentilla, Bloodroot.

Uses: Diarrhoea, Bowel inflammation, Intestinal parasites.

Description: The Tormentil herb is a member of the Rose family. It can be found all over Europe, growing wild in woods, moors and grassy pieces of ground. It is a small plant with yellow flowers. The root is thick and red on the inside, giving rise to the name 'Bloodroot'.

How it works: Tormentil has a high tannin content, which gives it a distinct astringent action on the digestive tract. Tannins bind to the proteins present in the irritated lining of the bowel, forming a layer which soothes and, at the same time, provides a barrier against infective organisms and toxins. They also slow down the frequency of bowel motions, encouraging the healing of an inflamed bowel.

When to avoid: Consult your doctor or practitioner if acute diarrhoea persists for more than 36 hours.

URTICA

Also known as: Stinging Nettle.

Uses: Arthritis, Gout, Detoxification, Allergic rashes.

Description: Urtica is the name of the Stinging Nettle commonly encountered on wasteland as a weed. It has, however, been treasured for a long time by herbalists as an excellent 'blood tonic'.

How it works: Nettle has a diuretic action, attributed to flavonoids which increase the excretion of a number of waste substances from the body, particularly the acid metabolites. This action is of particular benefit in gout and arthritic conditions.

Urtica has a nutritive value, containing vitamin C, iron, calcium, potassium and silica, which explains its tonic action.

When to avoid: Do not use if suffering from diabetes or blood pressure problems.

UVA-URSI

Also known as: Arctostaphylos uva-ursi, Bearberry.

Uses: Cystitis, Urinary Tract Infections.

Description: Uva-ursi is a small plant found in Europe. It has small peculiarly-shaped flowers, which some consider to resemble a bladder.

How it works: Uva-ursi has urinary antiseptic properties by virtue of a glycoside known as Arbutin. The way this substance works in urinary tract infection is unique.

Arbutin is absorbed by the body and broken down to hydroquinone and glucose. Hydroquinone is then excreted in the urine, where it exerts a direct antiseptic action in the kidneys and bladder. This action is stronger in alkaline urine so a fruit and vegetable based diet is recommended.

When to avoid: Consult a healthcare practitioner if symptoms persist for more than one week. Do not use if pregnant or breastfeeding.

VALERIAN

Also known as: Valeriana officinalis.

Uses: Anxiety, Nervous tension, Insomnia.

Description: This is a herb which is widely found across Europe. It is one of the oldest herbs in use and has been the subject of extensive research.

How it works: The tranquillising action of Valerian has been attributed to a number of components. The group of compounds known as Valepotriates have the ability to 'calm' the nerves.

The substance, Valerenic acid, inhibits the breakdown of GABA, a chemical transmitter in the brain, which helps to decrease activity in the nervous system, and this in turn can aid the promotion of sleep.

In addition, a number of other constituents in Valerian have been shown to possess antispasmodic activity on muscles.

When to avoid: Consult your doctor or practitioner if currently using other medicines for the nerves.

VINCA MINOR

Also known as: Lesser Periwinkle.

Uses: Impaired memory, Tinnitus, Menière's disease, Dizziness, Headaches, Nosebleeds

Description: Vinca minor is a perennial plant and a common inhabitant of woods and hedgerows. It was used historically for fluxes — bleeding at the mouth or nose, and for bleeding piles.

How it works: Vinca minor contains the alkaloid Vincamine in its leaves, which has an astringent effect on the tissues. Vinca minor works via its astringent/tonic effect on blood vessel tone throughout the body. Blood supply to the brain is improved helping memory, concentration and the alleviation of dizziness, making Vinca minor an alternative when Ginkgo biloba is contraindicated.

When to avoid: People with brain tumours should not use this herb. Do not use if pregnant or breastfeeding.

VIOLA TRICOLOR

Also known as: Wild Pansy.

Uses: Eczema, Non-specific skin rashes.

Description: This is another plant that is familiar to many people. Not many know, however, that herbalists have for many years taken advantage of its distinct action on the skin to help with eczema and other skin rashes.

How it works: Viola contains saponins. These 'soap-like' molecules are able to soothe inflamed areas of skin and, in part, are responsible for the soothing effect of the herb when applied externally.

The saponin content also makes Viola an 'eliminative' remedy. Blood flow to the kidneys is enhanced as is the elimination of toxins.

Viola also contains high levels of flavonoids which have the ability to stabilise capillary membranes. This is an important consideration in inflammatory conditions of the skin.

When to avoid: Do not use if pregnant or breastfeeding.

YARROW

Also known as: Achillea millefolium.

Uses: Indigestion, Digestive tonic.

Description: Yarrow is classified by herbalists as one of the bitter herbs. Other herbs in this category include Centaurium, Gentian and Dandelion. These have the common ability to stimulate digestive processes, increasing gastric juice secretion and improving the breakdown of food.

How it works: Yarrow contains volatile oils and flavonoids. These have an anti-spasmodic and anti-inflammatory action on the digestive system, easing colic and reducing flatulence.

Bitters stimulate the tastebuds. This triggers off a reflex nerve action which increases the flow of saliva and stomach enzymes. The sum total of this is an improvement in the digestive function of the stomach and small intestines.

Bitters can also be very useful for children with poor appetites.

When to avoid: Do not use if you intend to sunbathe or use a sunbed as Yarrow can have a photosensitising action.

INDEX